Calling from the Back Roads

Calling from the Back Roads

A Collection of Poems by

Kathleen A. Herrington

Published in the United States
© 2015 Kathleen A. Herrington
All rights reserved

ISBN: 978-0-9885927-6-6

Cover photopgraph by Kathleen A. Herrington
Book and cover design by
Booksmyth Press
Shelburne Falls, MA
www.thebooksmythpress.com

Dedicated

*to my mother, Opal Esther Herrington Ebest,
and my father, Harold Eugene Herrington*

List of Poems

Acknowledgements

With gratitude to Skip McCauley, Pam Reichenbach, Elizabeth Boutin, Sandra Humphrey, John Boutin, Mary Bombard, and Margaret Blanchard for your inimitable depth, your voice, your love of the arts, and for your support of this work. Knowing you, and being known by you, is pure treasure.

POEMS

Faith

More and more the thing that is you
is acquiring loose ends,
unraveling edges
where you find yourself slipping out,
as earth slips in.
Your body knows more than you do,
having come through the waves,
having climbed the grains of sand,
having lifted clothes from drawers
into the symmetry of socks in a suitcase.
Now that you've latched onto your thoughts
like a cat to a family of mice,
having decided what you want,
the path grows brambly,
your feet begin to bleed,
you long for a bed in the curve of the moon.
At first you think everything just is, of course.
When certainty fades and you're finally shaken,
a door opens into the field of no turning back,
and you enter there,
knowing your life is not yours to own
and nothing holds an own-ness
except the wheel and the one who turns,
even as the moon offers its crescent,
and the lions scream out their silver songs.

Root Land

Up from your bed like a red poppy,
you open to the sea of summer
and begin to consider,
is this the world you woke to yesterday,
sixty years ago?
A bee motors by in brushes of gold,
twirling your ears on waves of grass.
The silken drift of cottonwood lifts you,
and you jump the ties of a railroad track,
as if age had never passed.

Leaning over the river,
you watch a snake
swimming through places
you thought you'd forgotten.
Its head parts the water like a sliding zipper
and you hear the preacher say,
"Give them conviction while they still have life,"
and the snake flows into tree roots
and rests between two worlds.

It takes time to see this,
like what the river does with its catch of seeds,
and you feel the stun of a sight unseen
yet moving across the water
like something that would be known,
and you feel your childhood
like something that would not be lost.
You reach out to it,

and it comes to you as light,
traveling without its suitcase,
and you become wholly yourself,
and native to that place.

Coming Along

How could I think there was time enough?
The peepers have called and courted,
the snap of spring has turned to down,
and every butterfly has found its flower.

A little sign at the gate says "Meaning,"
and a voice murmurs, "Over here."
I enter holding an empty cup,
careful not to crush with my heavy step.

This time I'll ask no questions.
I'll break the bread and drink from the spring.
I'll know you by your heartbeat,
and we'll go together
into the untamed place called "living."

HERMIT THOUGHTS IN WINTER

I'm writing because you're you
and because the night air is so dark
and winter has become what I always thought,
a wild animal with silver stars in its throat,
the way we used to talk
and yet so different,
a hermit in blue scarves and a campfire coat,
asking the moon down to the woods
and disappearing in a cave of light.

In my living room, the strings of a cello
vibrate on flame-tipped air.
Outside, hardened snow rests against the house.
Absence surrounds the form
around which the past recalls itself.

An open window reveals the passing moon,
a crescent dove gliding through layers of dappled dusk.
Time is a shifting proposition.
To understand, we must cross over.
To enter, we must leave.

At my window, the moon is moving by,
her tail feathers floating in a golden point behind her.

EARLIEST OF EARLIES

Earliest of earlies,
the sky arrives in small birds
darting across the snow,
unaware of a face at the window,
gentile, immigrant, gringo.

This is one of the mornings,
palest light, slipping through slender trees,
barely clothed in amber blue.
The tea is ready on the table,
the page is all potential.

This is one of the mornings.
Oh lovely opening, answer to darkest thoughts.
The sky is shifting on the ridge, above the place
where a deer is leaving tiny hoof prints
in the snow.

ODE TO EMPTINESS

That bird, yellow and swift,
rushing through the open space
next to the house, the peony, the potentilla,
flying through a shudder of thunder
under ripping volts of current,
a thought vanishing over the hill,
wings folded to speed the hurry,
is disappearing every moment
and reappearing
in the perfect refuge
of emptiness.

FREE IN THE CASCADES

A bear cub was hugging the top branches
of a Douglas fir when we saw its mother,
watching us from a clearing in the timber.
Our car was parked in a clump of others,
three or four jammed together on the shoulder,
everyone staring and pointing.
She could have been like us, eager and curious,
but she wasn't.
She knew something we didn't know,
and while she was looking into our eyes,
everything changed.
I became a ruthless animal,
and she remained herself,
a mother who loved her child.
We drove away then,
and took no pictures.

Again, the Prize

You wake up,
and you know you've won.
You toast the bread, make some tea,
all easiness in the dawn. You forget you've won.
You sit in the pink and orange light,
watch the trees ink in against the sky.
Asleep that night,
you see something,
your life,
flying over the ocean,
opening and closing its wings
like a butterfly,
and it's there you remember what you won,
and you know the stakes are high,
even though you're only sleeping.

MUTUAL

The trickling call of a cooing dove
opened the ear of memory
and an old woman knew again
the scent of sun on purple lilacs
and she thought to herself
how like a garden
is life at any age.

Leaning back in a weathered chair,
she looked into blue space
above an earth of seed and embryo,
blood and bark, sap and skin.
Rooted in breath and beating heart,
she observed a sunlit cloud floating overhead,
its porous edges moving toward her
as if with bearing on her life,
and she let herself understand this
as if mutual attention were present,
hanging suspended in the yard
like a vapor that soon would leave
and she could not resist these thoughts,
residing as they did in a dream
whose borders she had already crossed,
and she inhaled the passing beauty of her life.

Looking in from the street anyone might see
an ordinary woman looking toward the sky,
and yet she was tumbling into the mind of God,
taking with her the chair and its contents,
the grass and all its constituents,
the birds, and the very air.

GIRL IN A KNEE-LENGTH SWEATER

Feeling like a northern hillside
after the last snows
have sunk deep in the ground,
I saw eternity in the pebbled light of spring,
striding the world
in the curve of a girl and her dog,
she in a knee-length sweater of speckled brown,
he in a coarse coat of russet and gold,
togetherness and ease
in time with the streets,
pausing outside the grocery,
one bending down,
the other looking up,
the air soft and round
as she asked him to wait
and vanished inside.

He looked anonymous
like any dog standing outside a building,
lifting his nose into the drifting scent of afternoon.

The leaves fluttered a little on their stems.
I gathered myself and stepped away,
knowing she'd return just as she left,
like eternity always does, without a ripple.

Have You Noticed

Have you noticed how a desert sky
can invite you up at dusk,
the moment you see it,
the second you let it in?
Standing among the cholla
with coyotes slipping around,
it uncorks cool air from the ground
and you lean into it
like a train traveling upward
with borders dissolving,
your feelings leaping higher and higher
until you're halfway gone and then,
as if you might not notice it,
the desert grabs you like a cat's paw
and delivers you into its presence,
vast and discerning
in the cool night air.

Food from the Back Roads

Sometimes we left everything behind
except a pan of brownies, boots, band aids,
ice chest and a little cash
so we could get to the Chisos
and tune our ears to the canyon wren
and once, the scream of a lion
at the foot of Big Bend.

We rode out to taste the West. Sat next to cowboys
who took no notice and ate with hats on, no two alike.
We walked the uneven ground of Boquillas
and dipped our hunger in fried tortillas.
We felt the dust and sun falling from us
as we entered the green shade of a pool hall
on the Mexican side,

none of us homesick because home was us,
wanderers between Zion, Chiricahua, Taos.
Spotters of thick tarantulas too cold to move
and cocoons of fog sliding into the basin.
We conceived ourselves eating Navajo fry bread
and bathing in mountain streams on our own,
camping out with bears and stars at 3 a.m.,
living as we did back then, on a diet of wonder
and tuna fish sandwiches.

Things We Didn't Talk About
for E.J.B.

Something is present that wasn't before,
as if reaching the river of a deep canyon
and standing alone on the sandy bottom,
looking up at the stars,
knowing I am of them but can't touch them,
because they've already burned through me
and sent me to this place,
sculpted by the river of first and last,
and it's who I am now.

The river flows underground and out to the sea,
transporting bits of me, grain by grain.
I wondered had you noticed this difference,
did it show, had you seen,
and if you know you're traveling too,
and do you think we're going by the same river.

We talked of other things and moved on with the sun,
but I feel you on the path behind me,
in the untamed rosemary at the corner
or laughing under the boughs of the pear tree,
and sometimes I feel your presence
in the spilling rain, touching everything.

Professional Development

Yielding to the press
of streaming guests,
drawn to the dining hall
by civilized need,
we staffers moved as one
to sit before a hundred plates,
delicately tucking our napkins in
to begin the courtship of knife and fork,
pausing to look up at a sea of faces
and coming back again to wet, secret joy,
doing what we do
until the doing was done
and I stood to say goodbye,
and hurried into privacy beyond the hotel,
a panting animal running to deep woods
where rain was falling into the soft pelt of earth,
and the mantra of hidden frogs pulled me in,
and we passed the communion plate
in the dark outdoors beyond the walls,
unrestrained and fully ourselves
in the uncivilized and wild.

This Ticket

You and I are entering a strange time,
the time that comes to all.

We have entered, it has come.
Oddly, there is no going back,
no way to push it off.
We find ourselves in it
and it in us.

We wonder who will be first to board the train.
It may be you, it could be me.
Will we say goodbye? Will there be time?
We wonder this as we say hello,
as if we're not also saying goodbye.

The tarot holds little interest.
The great mystery is now.
You. Me.
The country of now calls to us
like birds to the light of waking.
We have only to listen.
The voice of now is everywhere.
Oddly, it is enough.

When the good looks, the money,
and the evening kisses are handed out,
and someone says
there aren't enough to go around,
it's all right,
because the ticket says "Now."

I can look down at it.
There it is in my hand,
the living ticket,
not the one fluttering down the tracks
as the train pulls out.

Not that one.
This one,
this ticket here, now.

TERRITORY

I'd like to go for a ride in Kansas.
My father would be driving
and I'd be twelve again.

His legs are long beneath the wheel
and I can smell his skin.
He's saying something about driving a car.
We're on a winding road by the slow-down creek.
He says, "Be ready for emergencies,
ready to grab the wheel and steer."
I can't see his throat,
it's hidden behind the tie he wears.

He has his secrets
but I don't think to ask for them.
Who are you really, Daddy?
How do you feel about your life,
and why did you marry Mama?

What do you think of me,
and what do you want in the world?
Do you like me?
Who am I, do you think?

But I'm just riding along in the not knowing,
content in the golden afternoon,
relaxed in the deep territory
of the angles and curves
of my father's profile.

Waiting

Sitting among tall tombstones
I don't want to recall
how the air was thick with evening,
nor the way
the lightening bugs were lifting
in the field of succulent green.
I don't want to think about how or why
an open heart moves down to the jump-off place.

I want to remember the blue sea
lapping over the land,
slipping with outstretched fingers
over coffee-colored sand, leaving
wetness bubbling down through dark grains.
I want to remember the wild sea
calling to that other water,
the lagoon behind the beach,
its wind-ruffled surface rippling in light.

I want to remember the way it answers,
because the sea has come calling,
and that other water has been waiting.

Minus Time

The body houses its history in a holy place
where the past is a remainder,
sometimes humming, always holding,
until a secret day
when the body wrinkles under its load,
and you want to lie down
in your permanent clothes
and let sleep bring the ease of what is
in the content of dreams about who you are,
while the whole of everything
is moving to change in all its forms,
the human world,
the hummingbird world,
the salmon world and worlds of worlds,
all rising and falling in the Holy of Holies,
inside the gate
in a place we call eternity.

Simian Line

Forsaking the azure blue
as it bends down to touch the earth,
and the earth too, lifting in golden leaf,
a ray of sun slips between the wires and bars
and moves across the eyes of the captive
at the corner of Nicholson and D,
and there describes the humanness of my face,
the borders of my feet, the gate that closes when I leave.
Unknown is the other,
except in reflections of my presence,
and in this one thing only,
lies the heartbreak
of the world.

Two Sisters in an Orchard

We parked on the powdering dirt
and wandered through desert scrub
to let ourselves be surrounded
by a hot blaze of sunflowers,
six feet high and higher.
We took in their calm,
their yellow bearing,
their petaled heads
riding the narrow shoulders
of coarse, green water straws.

We lost ourselves in looking,
and the flowers too looked openly up,
straight into the Arizona sun,
as if they could never get enough.

An anonymous bug
rode a bead of sweat
down my neck.
Unhinged by heat,
a bevy of doves went amok
in a flap of underwing-red.
Color-trumpeting light led us farther,
then resolved in triangular red ladders
standing open under boughs of green
and crowns of ripe, round peaches.

We ourselves went red, yellow, green.
Desire sizzled like burning wicks to dynamite.
Our eyes met and we turned as one,
and raced back for cameras.

STARTING OUT

Secure as tiny crickets
in the deep grasses of night,
we children fell asleep
in the resonant sweep
of earnest voices
singing to Jesus.

When alleys were dirt roads
and lilacs grew wild beside the apple,
we entered the temple
of windowed dreams,
moving like moonlit zebras
through the evening trees,
leaving stripes of light
floating down the streams
of our mothers' laps.

Not knowing
the future
was on its way,
we awakened one day
to a grown-up's world,
our tiny clothes
still hanging in the sun
of a bygone beam
of happiness.

Prayer Meeting

Warm sidewalks waned into the pebble gray
of summer evenings around our house
while my family made ready for church
on Wednesday nights.
Resting my chin on the counter
in the dark of my mother's kitchen,
I waited, looking into the red-orange eye
of the radio,
privately listening to black-robed voices
chanting and urging, falling off and returning,
repeating through the glowing light,
"Holy Mary, mother of God, pray for us sinners
now and at the hour of our death, amen,"
over and over
until my father came to turn the knob,
and we stepped into the warm murmur
of our neighborhood at night.

Young Kid, Unforgotten

There goes someone, it might be you
but she looks like me,
a wavering flame on a skinny wick,
walking through empty rooms
where the family slept,
opening cupboards and doors
with a pounding heart
to see for herself
how absence looks.

Consciousness can come like a comet,
and it does,
to an old grove of memory
around the house she knew,
opening all the rooms
to a blaze of light,
the way the sky can turn to fire
when evening fills the air
and a train pulls out,
even as eternity is slowing down,
as if there is no illusion,
as if her family isn't on board,
and she wants to grab hold of that train
because she knows it won't be back,
and all her youngest feelings
are reaching for that old track.

SHAMELESS
for the S children

The old folks said, "Don't do what we did,
don't make those easy mistakes. Be happy, child."
This was the beginning, when innocence still held,
like a seed inside its jacket.
I didn't know what they were talking about.
Happiness was already mine,
and mistakes were no trouble.

Then came sixty years of appetite,
sixty years leaning into life
and floating too, like any twig on the river,
riding the leaping fishes when I could,
stopping at picnic tables along the way,
listening to train whistles
and curious things with tails, moving through the grass.

What can I tell you of appetite,
that it's a jumping fish, an ancient thing,
returning over and over again?
I could tell you what you'll find out,
that if you live, you will and you must,
eat your fill -- and only later
can you claim your truth.
Be happy, child.

So Far Back

We are here from so far back
we have no memory
of ourselves as animals.

I saw a man with a nose and two little eyes,
a mouth, some cheekbones and hair on top of it all.
He was driving a red pickup,
looking like he owned the truck, the road, his life.

I thought of a beady-eyed little mammal,
pocket-small, climbing through the trees,
and others crossed my mind:
red-winged dragonflies,
wobbly porcupines,
sunning lizards,
swimming turtles,
all peering out from faces,
having arrived after a time
when the earth was without form,
and darkness was on the face of the deep.

Looked back at the red pickup,
through the windows of my truck
into the windows of his truck,
where he was viewing the world.
A flash of intimacy passed through me,
not only with him but all these others.

A bumblebee looking at another bumblebee.
A swan swimming toward her baby.
A bear, touching another bear.
Me, looking at this man in a red pickup.

Undercurrent

On those nights
when you collapse yourself
onto the bed,
grateful to drift
between moonlit trees
and the occasional splash
of something
coming up for a breath
of glittering darkness,
one of your own thoughts
with a thin blue fin,
dropping deeper
and yet not deep enough
as a car cuts by your window
on the pebbled street,
and your raft-fin changes
into hot, tangled sheets
and you get up,
feeling your way down
to the bottom step,
where you open the door
to cooler air
and calling crickets,
and it's there you remember
the image you woke to,
a person you once lived with,
someone you could touch,

and the surprise
of finding a kingdom
of mutual understanding,
and then losing it,
and this is what brings you to your kitchen
to heat water for tea,
to sip it as you sit
in your late-night chair,
missing what is missing,
knowing you're not supposed to
anymore.

RETURNING TO KENT

In the long-ago of the four of us,
we giggled like children
in the radiance of morning
because we thought we were free
and that's all it took,
to be in the world
as if we were chosen,

and what could we choose
but the unbounded present,
heading west in a rented van
through the back towns of Texas,
stopping for tacos and border burritos,
leaning against sun-baked adobe,
soaking up happiness.

Yesterday on the sumac path
between a track of rail and rippling river,
the wet scent of summer weeds
took me under a bridge by a flickering pier

and there unfastened the memory
of a crumbling foundation
where we once stood in sunrise gold,
inside rock walls under open sky,
in the wilds of something old,

and I felt quickened all over again,
yesterday without my friends,
looking out from my own crumbling form,
itself going back to the wild,
still craving the light,
still a bold and wide-eyed child.

The Great Venn

Dotted with day lilies and blue iris,
the path to the meditation hall
led to a round body of golden brown fur,
a presence sitting on the road,
its eyes already on us, fully aware.

The you of the old familiar
and the you of new otherness
clearly saw it too.
You and I,
the I you knew, the I of now,
and you,
saw its eyes seeing us.

The grace of a falling petal I did not see,
but in the stillness of deepest red,
it has come to rest upon the table.

Journey

There she is, the one who smoked the medicine,
ate all the plums and lost all sense,
locked in the old present like a frozen bud—
believing she had time and forgiveness too.

A distant voice suggested accountability,
but she couldn't take it in.
She didn't know her every move would make a difference,
that every deed would be remembered
by, of all people, herself.

All she'd ever thought of was now, now, now.
Who could have guessed she'd live past sixty. Who knew.
Who knew that every little deed has multiple consequences,
the ones in the moment, and the ones to come later.
Now she's here in the rest of her life,
facing the future of the past.
She never knew she'd be one of the foolish,
and yet here she is,
dunked, bathed and dried in it.
Is there any hope? Will there be time to wake up?

Just this morning, impatience bloomed in her voice,
as if she knew who she was talking to, but she didn't know.
It was me. I've been here all along.
She wonders if it's possible to remake herself.
Self calling she.
Hello?

Lying Down with the Lilies

The opening peonies so lately young
reveal their dreams on pistil tongues,
and blue dragons lower their wings
to settle in the thickening sun,
while soft-shelled turtles line up to listen
as spring lies down with the lilies.

Honeysuckle vines lift up in tendrils
like slender prayers on rising currents,
everyone present in the field of a moment,
doing what we know how to do,

until the return of what is forgotten,
as dusk settles in like the past
and the water goes smooth
between the curving edge of purple
and the beginning of a new day.

RIVER

Looking over the trestle below the guard rail,
leaf on the river is riding the silver
but your love, Mama, is what I'm missing.
No pile of words can bring you back,
no easy glide on a hot train track.

When I first heard what rivers do,
I found one moving into mist,
barely believable there it was,
current to another side
where the past leapt forth
like a great fish,
up and down and out of sight,
luminous in the dark of night.

When the earth turns away from the sun
and clarity vanishes into evening purple,
I let the river roll into my rest,
peopled with lineage and impermanent death.

Tondo*

Sunlight passed through lifting sprigs of cedar
and the bamboo chimes began to tap
in the wild splendor of a tipping ta
as we taddled-oh
in the moving air of morning,
like two seeds aloft, we tangoed
in the taddling tondo.

Spring was on the water like a dipping paddle,
tapping out tenderness in tiny cups of tea,
splashing happiness over and under us.
Oh tee totaddle,
together we were,

I like to remember it,
the taddling tondola of tingling cymbals,
together with you oh tee oh ta
in the land of otta,
oh ta oh tee.

* "Tondo" is a Renaissance term for a circular work of art,
   as in a painting or sculpture.

Something for Sleep on a Hot Night

Coming from years away through thickets of death,
I saw you in touching distance of the sky,
picking berries on the hill.

Between my house and where we stood
were ticking clocks and back roads
and the sun's best stretch of hills by old Dave's place.

Trilling voices flowed from blueberry bushes
like singing song sparrows.
Your pail was almost full
and there was Mary in her coolie hat, and Lacey too,
with her little girls, Margaret Ann and Lily Kate,
all in sync with the sun, wearing long sleeves and cover-ups
like berry pickers of olden days.

I came to stand with you in a spell of remembered grief
but bent down instead to Margaret Ann
who took me into her dream of childhood
where rivers flow and seams undo.

I looked up to twenty crows rioting in the sky
and savored my footing in the presence of wonder,
seen by a child in the fresh wash of life.

HOLY, HOLY, HOLY

Overnight in the cooling stars and curling smoke,
unseen like a forgotten glass of wine
beneath the backyard oak,
you took your time
kissing every leaf and blade of grass
and in that way it's always you I'm missing
and if you would take me with you,
show me how you do it,
I would cross over and back again,
and sing the evening alleluias.

LAPIS BLUE

Daily chores drift by like pieces of kindling into the fire,
as if something is waiting just out of reach,
one act leading to another, as if completion is possible
and the thing awaited may soon arrive.

The earth turns into leaves lifting past the window
and the story of the angel comes back
in a blue lapis light,
talking as if you're talking to yourself,
listening like birches leaning into their own shadows.
When the wind goes cool in a vaulted dome,
and the angel comes down from the dark,
a figure walking toward you in hat and coat,
you realize how deep you are, inside the story.

Now and then someone asks for your papers.
Someone in a dream might say it
as if something is waiting just over there,
and you might know it like the click of a lock,
and you sense yourself animal in a perfect human body
when a voice gives utterance and the angel is present
like solitude in a dewdrop,
listening as if completion is possible
and the thing awaited will soon arrive.

Over time you recognize the landscape
and later you understand its size,
not just one or two fragments but sprawling and huge
and you realize your little story is *the* story,

your entire family and you and all of everything
are in it, and still later it's not a story at all,
it's your life, and it's nearly over,
and the blue lapis light is sitting beside you.

READY

Dappled with age,
they belonged to each other
like truth to truth
and knew themselves native
to places now passing.
The maple released its leaves
in the rolling smoke of an autumn breeze.
Shadows grew long on the backyard hill.
They tended their gardens, people, animals.
In the evenings, glancing at the moon,
they sipped their wine outdoors,
remembering old migration routes.

Love Note to a Muse

Like rain seeking passage
to underground rivers,
you touched me with your eyes.

Memory darts near the surface
like tiny minnows
while I sit on a park bench,
missing you.

The wind is wild like a great sea gust.
The day is hot.
The grackles stand unmoving in the bath,
their mouths open wide.

Home again and waiting,
I feel a rush of wind
blowing through the house
and out again,
bringing the river in a dream.

Black water laps at my canoe,
and I tie it to the deepest root,
going on foot to find you
in the ripening grass and
waking in the curve of your angel hips,
in a temple of open sky.

BACK THEN

I was alone in the car, waiting.
The evening streets were black with rain, and shiny.
Water droplets fell in soft pats on the gray roof.
I was watching from the inside, and waiting.
Raindrops streaked the windows.
My face lifted to the sky, and the sky came down.
Street lamps shimmered in points of light.
And then he was coming. I saw him.
His long legs. His big overcoat. Running.
The door swung open and he laughed to see me,
and we rode home together like raindrops to the river,
in my father's time, in the town where I was born.

Taproot

Home early from the day beyond my street,
sheathed in sunlight on my skin -- and even feet,
two cats investigate the residue
of all the lives I've been passing through.

Surrounded by the thick greens of summer,
we sit in Vermont like quiet lovers
while a tiny wasp
the color of butterscotch
lowers its feet to a forest of grass,

invoking the thousand wrinkles
of my father's mother,
her black shoes with black shoe strings,
and the putt-putt of an old motor
as I traveled the back roads
on the seat beside her,
content in the knowing of my grandmother
and the way the car opened the future
like a spreading happiness,

still here after all these years,
lit up like a meadowlark
in the green grass of Kansas.

BELONGING AS WE DO

Under the stillness of snow and ice,
between frozen banks of solitude
like feelings held in check,
the river knows its way.
Higher up the wind touches heaven
and drifts down through feathers of chickadee
and ladderback.

Under the white,
the water is saying to snow,
come down,
let me melt your cold heart.

Air currents dogpaddle by
and a snippet of joy comes splashing out
like an angel lifting off,
sidestepping the slick of ice and crunch of salt.

What are we if not the water trickling below,
belonging as we do
to the longing underneath,
and the fealty of the snow.

EARLY

Even as a beast is scraping its tooth
over snow-bound streets,
I slip from warm covers,
touching bare toes and soles
to a cold floor, undecided,
dwarfed by the roar of a second truck
spinning salt from its hindparts,
rattling its metals like tin cups on a cage.

Regaining momentum,
pushing feet through the gloom of boots,
capping my head in wool,
pulling on mittened gloves and jacket of fleece,
I will go out and taste my life,
outside in the animal air
before thoughts take over,
to stand with the others
and watch the trees take on color
in the rosy birth of morning.

WANTING TO TELL YOU

Lost in the heart of an overnight guest
are the feelings that want to talk,
having flown canyons with feathers outstretched,
to tell you the life it took
to see you again,
the meetings with owls and red-tailed hawk,
escaping from graves of centrifugal thought,
pushing out like a cicada leaving its husk
on the rough bark of an oak.

Looming around the edges
is something large and still, as if petrified,
and we know petrified wood
is no longer wood
but the minerals of surrounding eons
having rolled in,
saying this is the past
from which we must move.

CONTEMPLATION

The willingness to let someone new
come into your life,
to paddle their canoe between the tufts
of water grass
where your entire past lives,
can become a longing
when you wake to aloneness.

But if you do the unnatural thing,
if you persist in quietly sitting
on your back steps
with a cup of tea
and a cat,
the moon will sometimes
sit down beside you
in a halo of light.

And the light,
as we begin to know,
is just short
of reaching everything.

WHILE YET WE LIVE
in memory of Opal

When you were round like a water pearl
and my life was smooth and new,
I loved you first in time unmeasured --
the stories you told
of grasshoppers in tiny dresses,
the ones you'd made,
and how you sleep-walked through the trick of a lock,
and roamed the streets asleep at night.
There was time back then beyond the clock
to tell me everything.

While yet we live, we are a place, a dot of identity
in someone's head, larger than any day we've lived,
bigger than breath and deeper than nickel
in the core of the earth.
From a distance we feel each other,
latitude soul crossing longitude flesh,
two lives touching on tethers of air,
entwining and turning in space
like a braid of prayer.

Before you died I didn't know there was a net,
in and beyond my mind.
Back then, just a thought
could bring you as close as my own hands.
Strange I didn't see the sparking fiber then,
it's only now I know what holds
and in it,
what is not held.

As trees lose their leaves in the twilight of dusk,
I think I'll call you.
I forget you're not moving.
I forget I don't know where you are.
Life still swings its net and only some know
who it holds no more.
Only some know of its existence at all,
because too soon the net will leave us
like magic things stripped of our spell,
uncompassed by darkness
in an infinite surround of stars.

WHO KNEW BACK THEN WHAT HOLINESS MEANT

God said, "Tell me about your life, how has it been,
what is it like?"
Recalling cool air slipping along my skin,
how likeable as long as the silver key still turns,
I answered, "There was no hurry today.
I turned an inner tap and a stream of ease poured out."

It seems my memories are coming back,
how four good friends would talk on a sofa
and the chiming of bells
would bring the man from Mexico,
pushing his cart down the alley
toward home.

Deeper in the chemistry of hours,
the sky cooled to silver as we climbed cold stone
to enter Christmas at midnight,
sitting coat against coat on a wooden bench
in a stopping place between the ages.

As that which is no longer there
can come again to presence,
remembering appeared on the tongue,
and alleluias rang in the air.

At home those nights in San Antonio,
we slept in dreams of light
while the earth drew near the future
and the past became a star,

still visible here
where the sky speaks in snow,
changing the roads
and telling us slowly
how to go.

PICKING BLUEBERRIES

I'd been thinking again,
yet why should I say it.
Everything may go, so why tell.
I needn't, and yet I heard how it's a natural law,

how life itself is sitting
in a window of time
somewhere in the hall of eternity.
A young scientist explained it.
He looked into the camera and said
"The window is now."
I agreed with him there.
He said life may have a trillion years in the window,
but matter will one day go.
Be gone, is what he meant.
I felt a little depressed just thinking of it.

For half a second,
I imagined unredeemable nothingness,
and then two children appeared on the hillside,
barely the height of a corn stalk,
helping us pick blueberries
in the hush of the dream they were dreaming,
and as we bent down to talk to them, we entered that place.
It was theirs, but we could kneel in it.

When we stood up again,
forgotten things came to us in a kind of trust,
like rocking in a glider on a firefly evening,
as if everything would be and always was
all right in the ever now,
because children are with us,
dreaming their dreams,
and we grown-ups are standing by.

Who We Were

Cold Mexican nights in Texas
can take you to heaven
if it's the wallowing side of a weekend
and you're with the love of your life
eating home-made pizza
from a pallet on the floor,
watching movies and turning sometimes to see --
were you looking at me,
and falling then through the waves together.
You know how it is, don't you?
I mean under the covers, spoon to spoon,
with tree shadows on the walls,
sketched in by the moon,
tucked into a back yard
of hammocks and oaks
while the Gulf of Mexico glides over the Balcones,
relaxed in the fullness of life loving life.
Tomorrow can come, and it has,
but those nights in Texas
I want to remember
when faces and people have changed,
like a painting in motion until the brush goes still,
and the painting-filled-with-changes
is whole,
like a mountain turned valley
in which clouds are the signature
of a landmark gone by.

Wild Hill Road

Come see us, you said.
We'll be home later.
Take a left at the dirt road,
across from the orchard.
The house is unlocked.

The way the air parts
when I walk through your door
says pretense cannot hold here.
Your table is simple, carved from a tree.
Sliding my hand across deep grains,
I sense you as a waking dream.

Where the hidden has given up its mask,
the stairs are a deep red, the air is relaxed.
On the table, five plums of purple fill a blue bowl.

Your Last Gift

Before loosening out to rough waters
where the old whales swim,
I looked for identity in the roles I played
and every day checked the mirror
to see what took, and if anything showed.
This is what I've done in life,
this is what I did
until I saw you on your bed
unfastened in a fall, and I knew that
for you there would be no other story
and no more chances to be together
except this one, with forever
standing at your door.

A Thing So Old

The past is gone by

    but it's always changing.

        Coming to a close

            it seems to end

                but never its thread,

                    only its person.

                        Another person will come along

            and pick up the thread,

        never knowing

    they're picking up

a thing so old.

Gliding in on a Golden Leaf

Walking this new country where the sun comes softly
over milkweed meadows,

there is knowledge of a breeze
sighing through the backyard trees
of a former life.

Here, when evening takes hold in the distant hills,
a beast stands on its hind legs and howls.

In autumn, the past rises like smoke on the horizon
as grief glides in on a golden leaf,
bearing a scent of rot and fire.

APPOINTMENT

Having uncapped your jars of cover-ups and colors,
you lift your mirror from a bathroom drawer
and join your image with the coolness of cream
until you appear a little brighter
but your fingers can't find the buttons
on your clothes and you need a bath
except there isn't time because
you're quivering and almost blind.

In the car you say you feel like Little Orphan Annie.
I look at your smeared mouth and we laugh together.
We're on easy street now, heading for the dentist
like anyone might, and afterward we'll stop for dinner.

Home again, you're back in bed.
Identity slips into theory,
and I watch the moon roaming your house,
sliding off the edge of form. Red teapot on the stove.
Brocaid pillows on the sofa, night train
whistling through Tennessee.

ASKING

Lying down to sleep I talk to you the same
as when I was five and didn't know
how we live in jeweled light
where everything turns into its opposite,
and we don't know why or who we are
behind our names.

As if the end isn't definite and already in sight,
I lift my binoculars and look out to the woods,
the sky, the sea,
and death wears no visible color,
and I move on like a streaking rabbit
under the eye of something no one names.

At five I was completely young
but a long shadow leaned out across the ground
and found me, told me to hear the rattle of leaves
where change was shuddering in the light
and I ask now no differently than before,

if the end should come tonight
please take me in, let me live inside your robes,
and while sleep is coming, I listen for you through my skin.

Grandmother

When I went back to find your grave,
nothing was familiar.
Granite markers lined the level grass,
commanding every horizon.
I walked among them and called your name
until I spied a little orchard tree,
growing beside a broken sidewalk.
There on a stone was your name at my feet,
shocking the sky into tilt as I knelt
on the ground.
Grandmother of myself and mother to the land,
who knows your whereabouts now?
I thought you weren't there,
but as I turned to leave,
a rustling stirred the air,
and thirty doves hurried off
in the gray of November.

PRECIPITOUS

Driving
up the mountain of fog,
red tail lights blink out
and the road disappears
into muted distance.
The others
are dropping off the edge
and taking to the sky.
Like them,
I follow.

CAUGHT

We humans
believe in things,
water in pipes,
pieces of string,
the science of thought.

Ensconced in fixedness
like butterflies caught
in tacky stickiness,
we can't get free,
we won't let go

for fear of losing
all control,
and then of course,
we do,
gripped by conversion
in a common field
of unloosening
light.

PERCEPTION

Dreams can rise up like mist
and perish in only one night,
but a certain kind of death
can sometimes be undone.
The antidote is clear,
like a sip of hermit's water,
and tender,
the way an evening can settle in
like fog curling around a shore.

I thought I was moving toward the undoing
but the lighthouse bell grew distant and
perception began to change.
I listened from the bow of a moving boat
until the bell became a thin memory
and turning back lost all proportion.

Awareness can rise up like mist
and last a lifetime.
You are far away now
among dolphins and wet woods,
while I made landfall on another coast
in the campfires of a different life.

DAYBREAK

Attached to a fluttering heart,
I became a dream of silver light,
asleep in the dark on the passenger side,
with you on the left at the driver's wheel.

Drifting near the edge, you shifted down a gear
and when our car disappeared,
you carried us like a cloud, over sound and out of sight.

As morning opened and shape reappeared
we reformed in sweet summer air,
fresh from the trees, and we were home,
and unconsciousness fell away
into the curved pail of the fading moon.

CODEX

I always feel like a "me,"
one act dissolving into another
inside so many faces
I sometimes wonder
who we are.

It may be futile to ask
what's behind the behind,
across the across,
but if it's a secret
doesn't it belong to someone?

What if death is only a change,
and we never die.
It could be that everything is holy
and also a dream.

Something's been living here
for billions of years.

There it goes even now,
lifting in the wind,
walking with feet,
arriving in faces,
little me-cat,
me-snake,
me-woman,
prairie bluegrass
and maple,

lifting up
falling back,
you carrying me,
me carrying you.

Now feels like us,
and always,
I feel like me.

MENTOR BRIDGE
for Skip

When a dog's bark takes the shape
of a long "O" in the night,
and jeans pull up cool against my legs,
I find you leaning into a mountain of memory,
looking at me with steady eyes, smiling,
telling stories about your life and the
freewheeling women you once knew,
little details about what they'd said,
the way they walked, loose or tight,
and how you loved them because
they let you see them as they were
and didn't lie away their truth.

Standing still and traveling
at the speed of thought, I see us sitting
on uncut grass by the river, on the Kansas side.
You're reading to us, exactly like yourself,
taking us to a bridge so we can to get to
Dylan Thomas, T.S. Eliot, Cummings.
Lifting words from the page into a cloud of light,
visible in the water below us,
coming to us in a state of rapture,
a young man from the mind of James Joyce,*
staring at wild beauty in the form of a girl.
Your voice is true,
revealing something about who we are
and what might be done in life.

In an age when even the center was an edge,
I'm alone in your apartment, checking out
your books, your desk, your Murphy bed.
We're due for the night shift
and in you stroll, happy to see me.
You fill a coffee thermos, wrap some food,
pronounce yourself crazy, a lunch bucket Joe.
I laugh and we leave together,
crunching through a cover of crisp oak leaves
in the mantle of October,
all the while traversing the bridge.

Beyond those years, still half your age,
I wonder if you made it into an old man's skin,
and have you crossed yet,
into that unknown country,
or does your light still burn somewhere
in the wilds of Oregon.

*Joyce, James. *A Portrait of the Artist as a Young Man*. New York:
The Viking Press, 1964

ORIGIN

Behind the wheel
he looks through taxi eyes
like someone else
but he used to be a Sikh.
His story is fixed on an edge
like a sliver of carrot stuck to a wall.
Who would guess, days later, that its origins are carrot.
His are the thoughts of an overnight guest,
struggling to tell you of the road he has become,
his words no longer words but the minerals of another place.

Don't Want To

Like a tree
hiking into the mountains,
I too am slow,
and like air becoming breath,
I cling,
being vulnerable,
laughing so hard I cry,
fearing the approach
of the coming coffins,
because I've watched them
drop beneath the earth
and I know
I don't want to.

The Always Is

Like a clay pot
cooked in a kiln,
the feeling of always is
was here again last night

in a red-hot flame
pouring out from the center
like the warmth of music
in the middle of winter

when everything comes in
to the presence of always,
togethering itself
in the fires of the hearth.

This New Ground

In came the scent of salt and kelp,
over the dunes and trusting feet,
I remember how it felt,
as the cold ratchets out a notch
and the air bequeaths itself in snow.
I relax and strike a match,
and there comes a thud outside --
bringing a jump into a shiver
but I say it's only chunks of ice
crashing from the roof,
and the cats look up with eyes that say
"No such thing as only,"
and we blink together
in the thick of winter and settle again
into coulees of comfort,
one of us thinking how
all the other animals are still animals
except for the ones seized by a notion
and flung through the mind of creation,
even me, coming to rest in this place of snow,
at home in the heat of my body.
The cats are right, there *is* no such thing
as "only."

Good Bad JuJu

I had a ticket to the capital city,
a hotel too, with towels, television, a bed.
During the day, I joined the others for meetings
on how to brand ourselves.

At night, I looked through my window
to another box of windows
and thought I saw anonymity looking back.
But this may not be so.
Does a bug feel anonymous in a bug colony?
Perhaps I was mistaken.
Laughter trickled through the walls,
but I couldn't tell if it was live or televised.

On the second day, we listened to power talks.
A young man with coiled dreadlocks exhorted us
in jargonian, followed by an old man
who spoke in monotones about the ways of rules.
In the middle then,
the head cheese swept in with questions.
Branded answers and yes-nods vibrated through the air.
I sipped my coffee and wondered what I was doing there.
Was it the money?

Walking to the meeting that morning,
I'd seen the early sun
bending into a column of light on the sidewalk,
exactly where homeless people were lying
on a queen-sized bedroll,
nestled under blue-flowered sheets, asleep
as I passed by, on my way to a paycheck.

We were close,
like bears at the same tree rub,
separated only by the scent on our fur.

On Becoming a Hermit

The picture of children flying over the sun
was a little too high, so you took it down.
Your hair was a little too thick on your neck,
so you clipped it into the sink.
The grass was shorter than the weeds, so
you leveled everything.

The Passing Light

When the golden glow of a candle flame
leaps into shadows on the wall,
the understood can slip to a void
and words become a coyote's call.

Looking back on the life I've lived,
so many unconscious steps unfold.
How little then I understood,
the passing light we cannot hold.

O would that you will keep my spirit
and take me through the thing called time.
If love gives everything for your sake,
please grant requited love for mine.

Touch

To the one who would be true, she said,
"I am your possibility, awaiting none but you.
To know me, you must seek the sublime,
and leave the soft, side currents behind.

To find me, you must follow my voice
and if you reach me, there will be no choice.
We have only to touch and knowing will begin
in heart and lungs, eyes and tongue,

until we crest and part the waves as one,
slipping through secret coves completely open.
If you want to live, you must answer my call,
and I will rock you like the ocean."

For Nancy

The rain is falling
in silver wands
on rooted grass
and shining streets,
under the nether
of darkness.

The slender moon
is taking the train
down through the ground
on the sound of rain.
Sister—
can you hear it?

I'm going down fragile
to the dark interior.
I trusted the path to hold
and I'm going
to something not me,
down with the rain
and out to the sea.
Sister—
I can hear it.

STANDING UP

Leaving a long marriage
is like leaving your own species
for a life on all fours
where the unknown faces off
and looks only at you, faceless
beneath your childhood bed,

listening to the sound of light
falling like piano notes
on the figure of your father
as he watches from the doorway,
a knapsack on his shoulder.

If you think you're lost, Mama said,
life is a purple highway, lifting you
into the belonging air
on scooters of steady fire.

From your cocoon you pull a thread of silk
to join the father at the edges
to the mother, through the center.

Your skin touches a cool boulder
and you feel yourself trying to come home,
tucking in loose bits of fur,
building a campfire and laying out stones,
speaking in another tongue
that's now your own.

When you stand again in the woods of spring,
the forest floor is rearranged
and the old markers are missing,
as if something wild has just passed through.

Direction Home

There are memories stored in the body,
a scent of rotting leaves, changes in the light.
This is what they want to tell you,
like geese calling to each other in the dark,
when November comes with a hunter's gun,
do not hold out in that small fort
in what cannot sustain you.

When it's time to go,
ready your old trappings for the dead of winter.
Cart them like autumn debris to the nearest burn pile.
When it's time to leave, you can walk out free,
just open the gate, follow the sun.

INTO THE BIG

We found seats on a plane and flew over Texas,
just like that, to seashells by the ocean.
We offered a plastic card to the Avis man
and drove to Seattle in a green sedan.

Now we're hundreds of miles from all things usual,
the house we live in, our king-sized bed,
two cats and a backyard dog.

Where we are now is big,
and where we were before is a dot
at the small end of a telescope,
the backside of possibility
to which we're attached
by the grace of a thread.

FINDING FIRST THINGS

Stuck in love with a loss so deep
I almost dropped myself
from every bridge and hanging edge,
forever mourning, unable to stop
until I met you on a brink,
your hair flung out like a hundred watts.

We made a fire with sap and kindling,
we talked in color like an old-time dream.
You threw some ballast out,
I caught it piece by piece,
but my body sank another layer
down to where the floor was gone
and took me back to earth's old flesh
where I saw the ways of change
and recovered the kinship of balance
under the floating leaves
of late September.

Sometimes Don't You Want To

Sometimes
don't you want to give yourself up
and just be holy after all?
Roam around town
with an eye to others as you,
and you as all those others?

Do you not see through falling snow
how the stalwart trees go dark,
their bark sharpened in pencil white?

Do you not feel the mysterious air,
how it charges like a ram's horn,
taking you to stillness of woods
where the sun is making sequins
in the tops of trees
and traveling down
to the sleeping mosses,
quietly calling to none but you?

Lesson Fifty-two

Greater than I, the hand of fire
has dogged my path,
its touch has trailed my skin.
Mad with desire or barely burning,
I thought I was I and almost equal.
But not so fast.

When footsteps fall and no one comes,
midnight enters the heart
like the hush of October
in the listening leaves
when the moon turns over
in those colder mountains
of Vermont.

Even Now

By the river
of red and gold
memorias
there is a place
where water sometimes comes
and slips its kisses
down your naked legs
and slides your feelings out
like the toning of bells
on the delicate air
of early evening.

Daddy

When I was seven
and your name was "Daddy,"
you were home sometimes
and away sometimes,
but always in my head
like the prayers you prayed
from here to heaven,
little to big and back again,
time was passing, I was seven.

For twenty-nine years
we lived in palettes of change
but I knew your deepest hue
when I was seven
and you were forty-two.

A Reckoning

Lifting a jewel from the sea and treasuring it for a time,
did you throw it back and regret you'd done it,
did you blame it on the sea?

Descending the inner stairs,
memory raises its arms like a reaching child
and you know what you thought was yours
was only borrowed.

In a flash, the old paths are cut off by crashing trees.
From within the folds of bed,
a distant train passes through each ear.
Sleeping with one foot out the window and an old love
tucked into that puff of air called forever,
you find yourself in bed with a stranger.

Deep sea blue rolls in on waves of white
and you wonder if you have the courage to look.
The knower knows you will,
and who you'll see is yourself, familiar, waiting.

Coming Home

After many side turns, skips and reversals,
Christmas has bundled its holy space
into the frozen moon of January.
At the window, a single crystal, just a trace.

In the valley below, you're looking
at feather tracks in snow,
wondering what happened there,
but you know how it feels
to stand knee-deep in night,
your hat tugged tight against the cold.

The pull of Christmas took you south,
you're back in the north thinking it out,
you're not sure where you are,
but you'll trust the stars
to the crest of the climb.

Into the cave of your listening ear
comes the trickle of water
from a stream somewhere.
You draw your coat
around the slender tree
of your own backbone,
and lay another stick of story
on the camp fires of home.

SLOWER

Earth children don't like descriptions
of country gardens, meadows and rivers.
The mention of a single rosebud is enough.
Give them instead a story with speed.

But when they grow old,
they begin to drift toward the river,
and the river isn't enough.
The lives of a cluster of gnats
take on importance.
The skates on the feet of a water spider
glide into the present,
and light, shimmering through the trees,
causes them to tremble.

MAMA

Into the ear of dreams comes a knocking fist,
and I wake to you coughing on the other side of the wall.
Lying in the root-codes of childhood,
I hear the tiny deer stepping out
from the mosses around your house, slipping away
in the folds of night.

During the day you talk of simple things.
You're hidden in words flowing over a spillway.
I watch for you in the ripples below.

When I was once an aquatic breath,
you insisted me feet-first from your body,
and I discovered you among the bloody briars,
where unfeigned touch turned into trust,
and we belonged to each other.

Now you are ninety and your soft hair
is barely a covering for your head.
We sit among strangers on fold-up chairs,
six days after Christmas.

Minutes before the old year grows young,
night slips in and leads me out the door,
turning my feet into soft hooves
padding off to dark woods.
When I return, the year has moved on,
and you ask, "Where were you?"
I don't tell you I was outside, turning into a deer.

Now I'm fully human, feeling your pull in this airport.
The air is large with boarding calls and warnings.
Did I leave too soon? Did I see you? Do you know me?
The hands of the present transfuse my passage,
but the past is forever calling,
holding my heart
like a seashell holding the ocean.

OLD MUKTI DOG

Climbing up to the porch of evening,
walking through the open door,
we heard the sound of stillness,
the sound that follows a splash
when something drops below the surface.

Tiny rivulets of air rose up from the river.
Clothes were turning in the dryer.
As the ceiling fan hummed,
we felt our legs walking
like forked dowsing branches
to something lying on the floor.

Blue swathes of sofa mixed into edges of tungsten gold.
Sudden density lay in a heap at our feet.
Now, then.
Now, then.

Your small body is lying where you left it.

Mukti, climbing the hill.
Mukti, rustling the gates of grass.
You've gone and jumped the unknown canyon.
We weren't looking, we weren't ready,
and Mukti-oh-Muk,
we can't come until another day,
but all will be right
if you're waiting on that other side,
your dark hair blown back
from the thrust of our flight.

ONE OF US

Into the dawn scramble of momentum,
a dove's magenta wings fanned out in flight
and brought me the back roads of Kansas
in a vision of easy water on a slow river,
like the steady hand of my grandmother.

I crossed the bridge at 80 miles an hour,
glancing down to the grasslands below.
A voice flowered in my head as I passed over.
It said, "You are one of us."

A mile down the road, I smiled
and let up on the gas.

Someone We've Known, Someone We've Been

Who is she tonight, this woman in rimless glasses
reading alone, not young, not yet old, sitting on a sofa
that once sat elsewhere, new and untried.

She is silent, except for a page-turning hand,
and attentive, like a shepherd tracking each word.
Around her, a steeping story is swirling,
not the one she is reading, but another,
thick and demanding. She feels it seeping
into her bones, making her aware of her skeletal self.

As she reads, a curved cloud of air slips into the room.
Its cool edges pile up until she puts the book down
and consciously breathes them in,
letting memories of calling geese and wood smoke
contract in her throat.

A word of her own comes floating by: "Once."
The once of a little place in the woods
where she might awaken in a green tree trunk of windows,
a presence lying beside her, curious and warm
in the bed, coffee brewing in the kitchen.

Who would think this could happen,
a soul mate lying in her bed, yet she knows that it did.
Knows too, that 'once' is a word of sorrow,
a soft, golden purse
where moments are kept for second looks.
The cool air from long ago comes drifting in the window.
She breathes it in and lets the purse overflow
until nothing is left but to pick up the book
and start again.

September in Austin

Blue Pontiac LeMans
cruises alongside
like a parallel thought.
The driver blows a coil
of smoke
from his mouth, and
white trunks
of sycamore
lean up
as their leaves float out.
Behind the wheel,
he is sipping from the lip
of an amber glass,
his nose and chin almost touching,
his left hand a dried tobacco leaf
clutching a brown cigarette.
We sail together
under the sky's blue eye,
he concentrated and older than air,
I loose—yet growing wise.
I slow down to watch him pass
and the words
"Delivery Car"
streak by in a flash.

POEM OF CROW

for P.J. Reichenbach

Dark shapes of juniper and mesquite
bordered the clearing around your house
where the caliche path
curved back to the main road,
like a white snake in the moonlight.
Shifting pebbles spoke the sound of goodbye
beneath our feet,
and when the tires began to turn,
you jumped on the running board
to coast with me, past the eyes of deer
and clear discernment.
We listened to the cry of a nighthawk,
and you waved your hand for me to stop.
Your hand was made of moonlight.

We paused a moment on the road,
engine running, while you stepped down
to give a parting look.
We were old friends, and I knew you fully then,
within the current of that flashing brook.

RECOGNITION

That was her at 3:00 a.m.,
old on her feet, and wobbly,
wearing a pink pajama top
with all the buttons popped off.

There she was in the hour of difference,
teetering in a skin of dried daytime
almost deaf and practically blind –
a trickle of energy slipping through space,

all things done now,
nothing erased, and quivering,
like a mountain under gravity,
everything finished except for the child,
who was yelling, "Don't fall, don't fall,"

the two of them not even people then,
just a gaping gaze of terror
and a voice steering and calling --

she didn't want to fall --
"You can do it, come this way,"
as death pressed its paw
into her tracks,
"Come toward me, this way."

One more step
and then another,
until she dropped into bed, safe,
still my mother,
absolved at last of every grievance
by the child no longer a child.

POSSIBLE

Fear comes in a dark shape to the window.
We listen for the click of a shoe,
we believe the doorknob will turn,
and so we watch the news
because we think it gives an edge,
and if we watch for clues, there may be time.

Yesterday's story soaks us
with a national hero's sex life.
Tonight he apologizes to the masses
for being unfaithful to his wife.
We listen to reports of the latest bomb,
followed by interviews with victims one and two,
and we hear China is miffed
by the president's meeting
with the Dalai Lama.

Iran delivers an Iranian story,
we tell another from the West,
China teaches a Chinese story,
and none of them mesh.
Our presidents speak in lies,
our military talks in tongues.
We live among liars,
and we ourselves are fabricators,
not knowing what is real nor who we are.

In the narrow space between things visible,
something is saying we've come not for this,
but to begin to live what it is to be honest,
and to wake to the invitation of morning,
opening in golden ochre before our eyes,
offering unwavering purchase—
like our own centering hands
on a wheel of spinning clay.

Undiminished

From a distance
comes the great hello of winter,
addressing air and river ice
in sparks of light on untouched snow.

From a wheelchair
someone's voice pitches forward
in resounding waves.
"Hi, Hi, Hi."

Everyone is out for the thaw,
walking their dogs and pushing strollers,
showing skin, jackets open,

and the "hi" tone comes closer,
reaching my ears like the boom of a drum,
braving the dripping spray
and wading every puddle,
until at last we arrive,
eye to eye.

He looks at me and says
"Hi,"
and I merely wave
and he laughs,

two grinning fools crossing paths,
his voice a last touch to the hat,
a frozen howl rolling into the blue horizon,
content with wheels on a coasting chair --
because they turn the hands of a clock --
curling forward to meet the rise
of that which falls yet circles back.

TOGETHER

After the flood entered the plumbing,
forcing brown water to the top of a toilet
in puddles spreading beyond the door,
it fell like rain through cracks in the floor
and down again to the basement
where I stood subterranean in the grip of meaning,

thinking of source and burrowing bacteria,
reaching for buckets, brushes, rags.
Clean up could be done,
and I would do it all day in dripping sweat,
believing in possibility
and holding control in the palm of my will,

true to the task until I collapsed
in shorts and a shirt on an Adirondack chair
in a tumble of bones like a falling dead thing,
my feet bared to the grass, hat pulled low,
awareness gone slack until something crawled
on my outstretched legs
and I looked down at a skinny fly
moving along on its own thin legs,
bare-footed like me in the afternoon sun.

And I succumbed to the tickle of the fly and her friends
as they made harps of my legs and themselves the players
in a miniature orchestra moving from construct to tantra,
giving rise to rapture in shivers of bliss
for which I offered my all-out thanks
to the humble and lowly, the unloved yet holy,
darkly delicate and sensational
fly.

SURRENDER

Believing it unlucky to start a New Year alone,
I forever maneuvered mine into folds of human safety
until at last, undone by Christmas,
I stood solo in the threshold.

The house on Clarendon went dark.
The I and me slipped into petals of bed,
and beyond the frosted window pane,
night settled deeper than zero.

Is happiness always a surprise
and does it come uncalled?
I do not know.

On this eve of endings though,
I sank into the cup of the Big Dipper
and listened to space speaking my name
and felt myself pouring through a ladle of sparks
from which the New Year soaring came.

In the Moon of Apples

If the antlered trumpets of Colorado
were blowing the smoky edges
of October
and the light lifting from trees
like the cooing of doves,
and if I could hear the splashing stream
around a hundred galloping hooves,
I would not be old,
not when autumn has yet to quiver,
and still to call
are those lines of Keats, like leaves
that twirl and fall
around my cabin door.

The Two Things

Before tattoos were commonplace,
he showed me two things from his Navy days,
a small image of a fly on his left arm
and his fat photo.
The person in the picture
looked nothing like him.
Roundness spilled over a chair
in plump folds of permanence.
He said the vodka had been responsible.

And yet, he was here in the trim present,
wearing untried innocence
and a freshness in his clothes.
The fly was the surprise,
sitting on his lean, brown arm.

About the vodka I don't know.
It was Tom in the picture though.
Thomas Henry Webb.
A friend of mine from long ago.

Two Sightings, Northern Cascades

A gust of gray and snowy white
came whirling down the spruce,
fresh from the sky,
with a hooked, yellow bill,
landing on the railing
in pink, webbed feet,
head cocked toward us,
peering into our room,
asking please
for something human.

—

We looked into water so deep
it returned shades of blue and
no other, except
the silver of tiny trout
just out of eggs, no
parent about,
swimming together through blue.

What Lies Between Us

Months have passed and I want to call you,
buy a ticket and fly the mountains
to see you, push open the glass doors
and saunter down the hall --
into the red glow of your room
where you'll be sitting on your bed,
dressed and waiting.

I'll say, "Let's go have a milkshake,
or I can get carryout,"
and you'll smile and say,
"Bring us something."

The oxygen machine will keep time
from its place in the corner,
ka chunka, ka chunka,
and your records will lift violin timbres
over the ticking of bedspread roses.

I'll leave and come back with bags of food.
We'll sit across from each other, you in your chair
and I in mine, our sandwiches and chips piled
high on the little table, small and spare.

You'll be glad I'm there,
and we'll be happy together, and simple.
And then, not always in this way,
I remember that December,
and how you are no more.

Site of the Oppo

As rain fell through the morning,
I worked through the turning of the light,
twin-hands stopping time and keeping time
until darkness slipped through my fingers
and a thought arrived
that you've begun to sense me
in ways I cannot track --
the distance of an interior lock,
the other of me,
the flipside of you.

Oh would that we could accept
the parts that most offend,
we might posit our opposite together.
If indeed I did wound,
oh would that I had not,
and that is the rub of the sticky lock,
because I know not what you saw
from the other of you
to the flipside of me.

Oh that the antimatter could be embraced
by the matter,
that for which we long could belong.
Wanting to be loved and loving as we do,
the difficulty confuses

and we fall through tones and colors,
dropping away through distance and time
until at last we fall in
with the honest rain and its silver feet,
walking us home again.

When the Geese Line Up

The rolling call of the locust song
rides through the waving heat
and out to the sea of summer.

Its rhythm is familiar, like home,
and you wonder, is old-time innocence real?
Did you lose it?
Or did it leave on its own.

The days are passing in shifting light,
and when the geese line up to go,
you want to follow south
but you know you won't.

A voice says you are reaping now
everything you've sewn.
The time for sewing is past,
and you will not again be casting
in those fields,

and you might ask,
can I not realize it another way,
oh let me find another way.

And the voice answers no,
you are here for the harvest,
and it is here you will stay.

There is a Stone

Spinning through the green gold of childhood,
pitched like a long, slow ball from another time,
it coasts across steeples of amber grain
and picks up speed
to the tune of America, America
before it falls to land somewhere
in a company of bodies
lying still on the ground,
stalked by a stone.

OLD QUESTION

The body draws near what it's made of,
slipping through openings dark and invitational,
hungry for humus and teeming river mud,
touching with bare hands to fathom origin.

Coming home today I knew again my crazy love.
Pink-white clouds crossing curves of mountain green,
and red-winged blackbirds calling from the fields.
My love traveled out like photons of light,
unfastening tiny cells and organelles.

Do you think being in love this way is easy?
It is not easy, and it is what we want,
this grand delirium –
even as whole families are passing steadily away,
and certainty grows thick.
The earth will take its body back,
and what then, takes what is left?

Looking Out

Bending sweetgrass leaned over the place
where the cherry stones had fallen,
and spreading everywhere
were the softening hues of autumn.
Looking out of her house
like any of earth's old children,
she felt the weight of the season.

Her last words came while the light was changing,
the way it can when the leaves go cool and the wind
takes them off for a ride.
She watched them flying in a cascade of seeds,
winged and wild,
and when a leaf came to rest in her open palm
she took a breath of autumn, and she was gone.

We used to see her walking bent over,
down the streets of that Vermont town,
carrying depth on her shoulders
and distance,
like a ray of moonlight in the woods.

POST CARD
for the land people

Being with you for a day and a night
was like the wind moving down a mountain,
catching the scent of meandering light
and woodsmoke,
a deep draft from a seasoned pipe,
and for the span of a floating leaf,
a swell of harmony stopped everything,
and nothing.

Back in my own country,
I put on a soft cotton shirt
and recall
how like a wave you looked,
offering a hymn to the earth
with your hands,
and how at home I felt,
walking your path of sunlight and leaves.

The All Clear

Into the crawlspace of darkness
comes the carol of speckled starlings
from a gathering place in the pines.

Too long confined, the inside turns out
in naked skin and knee-high boots.
The March breeze swirls over patchy snow
and budding tips of green rise over
the fields like a born-again beau.

Leaning against the warm buffalo of earth,
riding the grass herds of simplicity
like a shouting outside wonder
or a quiet pudding,
cooling on the counter,
happiness flows in on a current of air.

Prayer to the Earth

for M.M.B.

Moving all day in the circling light,
a life, blinking on its own shy surface,
comes to a stop and wonders.

Am I doing enough to tell you how lovely
I think you are
to lay me down in your curving hills the way you do,
like an animal,
to drink.

There may come a time
when all love of you seems to cease,
but like water in the memory of dry land,
it shall be underground.

As long as you are in the world, I'm not alone.

No one carries the rhythm of the river
like you do.
No one else sings the old songs
and feeds me blackberries plucked from the bush.

When I nearly drowned, when the waves
rose over my head,
I looked in your eyes and you were there, looking back.

You listen like a shaman waiting for rain.
That's why I tell you these stories.
Who else can see behind the words,
the way you do.

Who else knows how to call me back
when the silver cord stretches out so thin.

Come with me to feed the hunger,
and I'll meet you at the harvest.
Tell me your dreams and I'll wade
with you out to the middle.
Come with me through the underground
and I'll loan you my body.

As long as you are in the world, I'm not alone.

TRUST

Sitting on the edge of the headlands in Maine

we rose together and coasted over the sea

and only later did we fall back to our bodies

on the sunny ledge, thick with strangers and

the now of noise, but you held the spell

and offered me a drink of fresh water,

and this is how I trust you.

Of Water and Rock

The hand of the sea comes easing
over the sand like a knowing lover.
Magenta-wet murals emerge from the rocks
on this not ordinary day.
It is the last day and foam spills from every edge.

Lying all about is a sprinkling of trust
in a feeling that everything is all right.
The open sea washes over the shore and
leaves itself in lingering pools.

My heart opens to a voice saying
"Over here. Come over here."
Sea sculptures stand up in prehistoric message,
smiling to us in saltwater and rock.
I hadn't known everything could be all right
until everything was.

UNEXPECTED

After all the people who've looked in our eyes,
the perfumes of earth, the pigments of sunrise,
the dim realization of death
like a repeating surprise,

I want to know where we went,
after the easy way the sun came shining,
and how we received it,
reaching through winter like the
white branches of a sycamore,
and how we listened to the tapping
of the talking rain,
going together into our depth.

After flying over houses and valleys
in our dreams,
floating down desert mountains
in the chasms of night,
after hearing a cry in the wilderness,
and realizing it came from us,
I understand,
and forget what I understood.

Finding nothing ends as I thought it did
and nothing begins as I believed,
I come at last
to the house of transition
where the secret wildness of life
places its stamp on me,
and makes of me something undreamed.

COLOPHON

This book was composed using
Adobe Garmond Pro
for both the poems and the titling at
GINGER CAT'S BOOKSMYTH PRESS